GREAT DISCOVERIES & INVENTIONS
That Improved Our Daily Lives

For a free color catalog describing Gareth Stevens Publishing's list of high-quality books and multimedia programs, call 1-800-542-2595 (USA) or 1-800-461-9120 (Canada). Gareth Stevens Publishing's Fax: (414) 332-3567.

The editor would like to extend thanks to Randall Farchmin, science instructor, Milwaukee Area Technical College, for his kind and professional help with the information in this book.

Library of Congress Cataloging-in-Publication Data

Casanellas, Antonio.
    Great discoveries and inventions that improved our daily lives / by Antonio Casanellas; illustrated by Ali Garousi.
        p. cm. — (Great discoveries and inventions)
    Includes bibliographical references and index.
    Summary: Explains the operation of common devices such as the doorbell, alarm clock, photocopier, radio, television, and computer; includes instructions for science experiments relating to these.
    ISBN 0-8368-2586-1 (lib. bdg.)
    1. Inventions—Juvenile literature. [1. Inventions.] I. Title. II. Series.
T48.C37   2000
609—dc21   99-053260

First published in North America in 2000 by
Gareth Stevens Publishing
A World Almanac Education Group Company
330 West Olive Street, Suite 100
Milwaukee, WI 53212 USA

This U.S. edition © 2000 by Gareth Stevens, Inc. Original edition © 1999 by Ediciones Lema, S.L., Barcelona, Spain. Translated from the Spanish by Grahame James Evans. Photographic composition and photo mechanics: Novasis, S.A.L. Barcelona (Spain). Additional end matter © 2000 by Gareth Stevens, Inc.

Printed in the United States of America

1 2 3 4 5 6 7 8 9 04 03 02 01 00

Gareth Stevens Publishing
A WORLD ALMANAC EDUCATION GROUP COMPANY

Clocks and Watches

Clocks and watches operate mechanically, electrically, or atomically. Most clocks and watches in use today are digital electrical clocks. Through the use of LEDs (light-emitting diodes) or an LCD (liquid crystal display), the time is displayed in numerals. A digital clock works because of electrical impulses created in a small piece of quartz or an electrical oscillator circuit. The impulses measure the passage of time. Mechanical clocks were once very common. The majority of mechanical clocks are powered by a spiral spring — a steel strip that coils up. When a mechanical clock is wound, the steel strip becomes a coil. As the coil unwinds, it turns a rod that is connected to a gear.

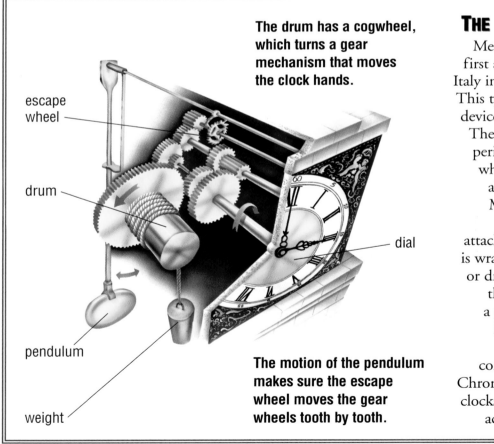

The drum has a cogwheel, which turns a gear mechanism that moves the clock hands.

escape wheel

drum

pendulum

weight

dial

The motion of the pendulum makes sure the escape wheel moves the gear wheels tooth by tooth.

THE MECHANICAL CLOCK

Mechanical clocks probably first appeared in the north of Italy in the fourteenth century. This type of clock contained a device called an escape wheel. The device marked constant periods of time, causing the wheels in the clock to turn always at the same speed. Mechanical clock motors contain a weight that is attached to a cord. The cord is wrapped around a cylinder, or drum. The weight makes the drum rotate and turn a gear mechanism, which, in turn, moves the clock hands. The timing is controlled by a pendulum. Chronometers, or very precise clocks, enabled ships at sea to accurately find longitude.

DIGITAL WATCHES

Digital watches have integrated circuits, called chips, that count the vibrations of a small quartz crystal. These vibrations are very precise, enabling the apparatus to keep time.

WATER CLOCKS

Time can also be determined with water clocks. The pointer the statue is holding moves up and down to indicate the time on the lines of the cylinder. Every hour, the cylinder turns slightly.

hammer

bell

spring

alarm release mechanism

catch

hour wheel

minute wheel

winder

main-spring

great wheel

MECHANICAL ALARM CLOCK

When an old-fashioned mechanical alarm clock rings, the hour hand has pushed the catch. The force accumulated in the spring moves the hammer from side to side to sound the alarm.

escape wheel

gear train pinion

balance wheel

balance spring

The Doorbell

The doorbell seems like a simple enough machine. Push a button, and it sounds. It is, however, a complicated mechanism. It works because of the magnetization of an iron bar that has an electric cable wrapped around it. Inside the doorbell mechanism are coils with an iron core. When the doorbell is pressed, these coils connect to the electric current, which magnetizes the iron core. This then draws back the arm of the hammer, which hits the bell. When the arm moves, the circuit is disconnected again. The iron core is then demagnetized. A spring moves the arm back again, once more connecting the circuit.

DOORBELL

When the electric circuit is connected, the electromagnet draws back the hammer, which disconnects the circuit. The hammer then returns to its normal position and connects the circuit again.

This crane *(above)* uses an electromagnet to pick up scrap iron. When it comes into contact with any iron, the electromagnet is activated, which makes the iron stick to the electromagnet. When the iron is ready to be dumped, the electromagnet is demagnetized, and the iron falls.

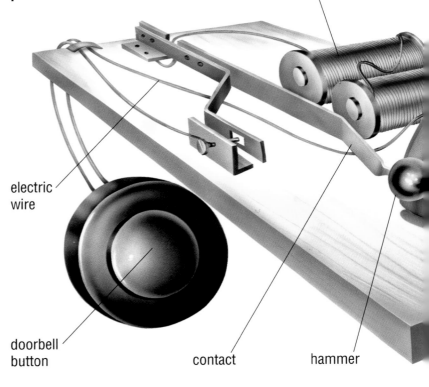

electromagnets
(coils with iron core)

electric wire

doorbell button

contact

hammer

MAGNETIC FIELD

Hans Christian Oersted discovered that electricity creates a magnetic field around itself. Other scientists like André Ampère studied this discovery in greater detail and managed to artificially create magnetic fields and magnets. Michael Faraday showed that a magnetic field could produce electricity. He carried out an experiment to show the relation between electricity and magnetism. By putting a permanent magnet in the form of a bar inside a cylindrical coil of insulated wire, he demonstrated that the bar moved when an electrical current passed through the wire. By the end of the nineteenth century, electricity began to be produced on a large scale for everyday consumption.

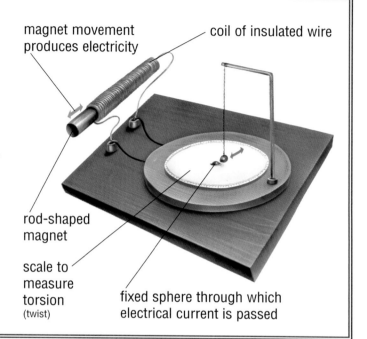

magnet movement produces electricity

coil of insulated wire

rod-shaped magnet

scale to measure torsion (twist)

fixed sphere through which electrical current is passed

When not in operation, the hammer takes the position shown in the diagram.

ELECTROMAGNETISM

In 1820, Hans Christian Oersted discovered that electricity moved the needle of a compass. This meant that electricity could produce a magnetic field.

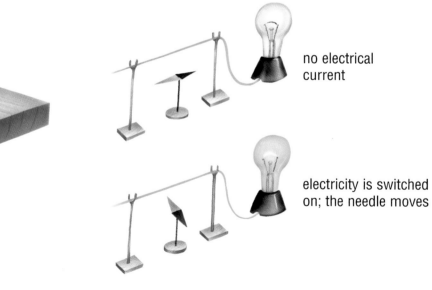

no electrical current

electricity is switched on; the needle moves

bell

The Photocopier

Some photocopiers use the properties of static electricity to reproduce documents. The copier contains a plate or cylinder covered in selenium, an element which can be charged electrostatically. A very powerful source of light is focused on the document to be copied. The image of the document is reflected and then focused by a lens that projects it onto an electrified selenium cylinder. There, a powder, called toner, sticks to it to produce the image for photocopying. The toner is then transferred to the paper and glued there by heat. Today, instead of a selenium cylinder, nearly all photocopiers use a plastic film that loops around rollers.

The ancient Greeks realized that when a piece of amber (fossilized resin) was rubbed with wool, it attracted lightweight objects to it. This was the first practical knowledge of electricity. The word *electricity* comes from the Greek word *electron*, which means "amber."

WHAT IS STATIC ELECTRICITY?

When one object is rubbed across another, surface electrons with a negative charge are transferred from the rubbed object to the surface of the object that is doing the rubbing. The rubbed object is then positively charged. Occasionally, the opposite may happen. The machine on the right is used to produce static electricity. With a turn of the handle, a piece of leather cloth is rubbed against a glass cylinder. This produces static electricity, which the metal "comb" then collects. The electricity can then be transmitted to a capacitor to be stored.

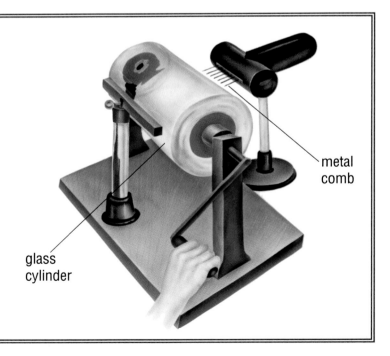

metal comb

glass cylinder

PHOTOCOPIER

cover

document

image is
projected
here

paper
tray

selenium cylinder —
areas exposed to light
lose their positive charge.
Remaining areas appear
in black.

paper
outlet

lamp

mirror

lens

heating
rollers

rollers   toner   drive
belt

EARLY ELECTRICITY STORAGE

Using a device called the Leyden
jar *(right)*, electricity can be stored
by connecting the metal piece in
the insulated cover with a current
generator. The jar, containing
water and lined with tin foil, acts
as a capacitor to store electricity.

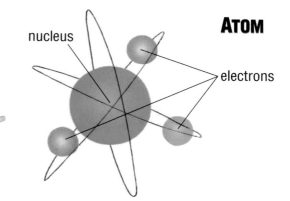

A STATIC CHARGE

Rubbing two objects
together *(right)* tears off the
electrons that are moving
farthest away from the
nucleus. They then pass
from one object to the other.

ATOM

nucleus

electrons

The Transistor

The first time the human voice was transmitted by radio was in 1906. The voice of Professor Reginald A. Fessenden was broadcast in the United States. With the use of a microphone, the sound of his voice was converted into electrical impulses that generated variable sound waves. The sound waves were then reconverted into sound by a loudspeaker. One of the greatest innovations in radio technology was the invention of the transistor in 1948. Transistor radios are available in extremely small sizes. Because they consume very little power, they can be operated with batteries.

FREQUENCY ALLOCATIONS

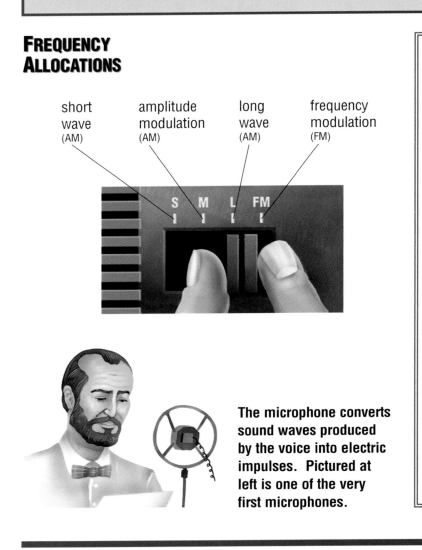

short wave
(AM)

amplitude modulation
(AM)

long wave
(AM)

frequency modulation
(FM)

The microphone converts sound waves produced by the voice into electric impulses. Pictured at left is one of the very first microphones.

VACUUM TUBES

Radio was able to develop because of devices known as vacuum tubes. Diode tubes receive the waves, and the triodes amplify the weak signals so the sounds can be heard. Before the appearance of the transistor, radios worked only with triode vacuum tubes. They were extremely fragile, were complicated to make, heated up slowly, and used a lot of electricity.

diode   triode

RADIO TUBES AND ELECTRICAL COMPONENTS

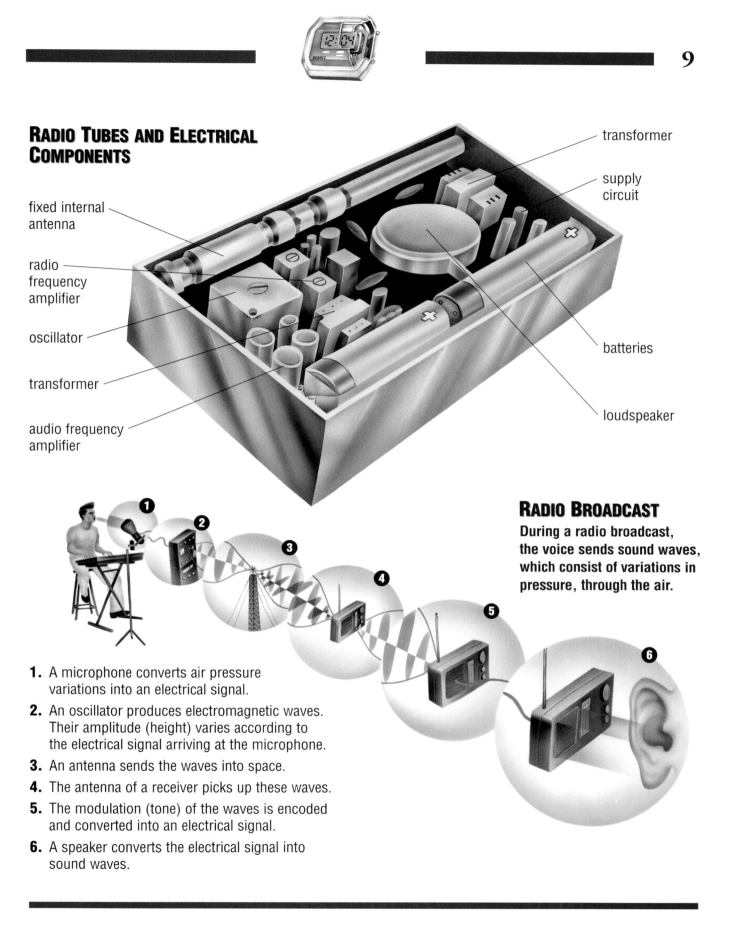

transformer

supply circuit

fixed internal antenna

radio frequency amplifier

oscillator

transformer

audio frequency amplifier

batteries

loudspeaker

RADIO BROADCAST

During a radio broadcast, the voice sends sound waves, which consist of variations in pressure, through the air.

1. A microphone converts air pressure variations into an electrical signal.

2. An oscillator produces electromagnetic waves. Their amplitude (height) varies according to the electrical signal arriving at the microphone.

3. An antenna sends the waves into space.

4. The antenna of a receiver picks up these waves.

5. The modulation (tone) of the waves is encoded and converted into an electrical signal.

6. A speaker converts the electrical signal into sound waves.

The Compact Disc

Thomas Edison was the first person to record sound and then reproduce it. This was possible because of his invention of the phonograph, which came before record players and compact disc players. Up until a few years ago, sound recordings were made in grooves (vinyl records) or in electromagnetic variations (tape recordings). Recently, however, the use of the compact disc has become widespread. In the compact disc process, sounds are encoded digitally. The process works on a system of two numbers: 1 corresponds to "impulse" and 0 to "not impulse." Every signal is translated into one of these codes and is stored in small tracks on the disc. Later, each signal is read by a laser beam, and a perfect, distortion-free reproduction of the sound is produced.

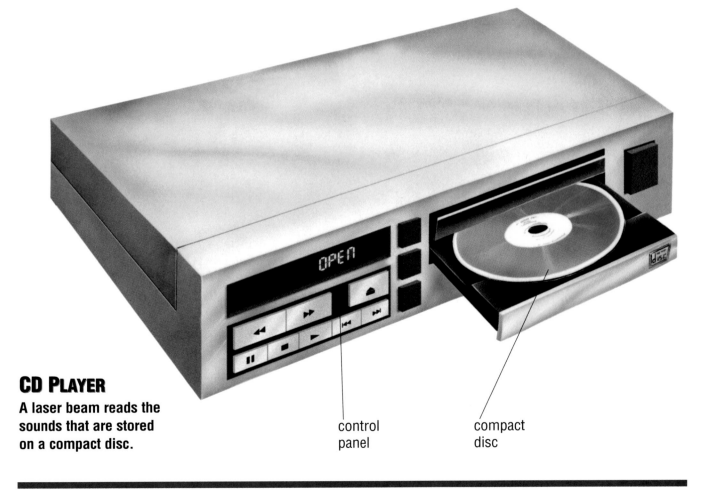

CD PLAYER
A laser beam reads the sounds that are stored on a compact disc.

control panel

compact disc

COMPACT DISC PLAYER

A laser beam is projected underneath the disc. The laser beam is reflected through lenses to a semiconductor sensitive to differences in light. It then reads the recorded sounds. These sounds are amplified and sent to loudspeakers.

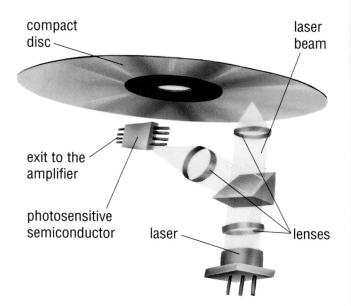

compact disc

laser beam

exit to the amplifier

photosensitive semiconductor

laser

lenses

HOW DID THE FIRST PHONOGRAPH WORK?

Thomas Edison invented the phonograph at the end of the nineteenth century. With this system, sound was recorded on a wax-coated cylinder. To reproduce the sound, the cylinder was placed on the phonograph and turned with a hand crank. A needle transmitted the voice vibrations to a thin disk, or diaphragm.

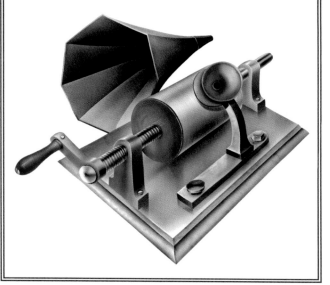

CASSETTE PLAYER/ RECORDER

The sound broadcast from a cassette player is produced by electromagnets in the heads of the cassette player *(right)*. The electromagnets read the information that is stored on the tape.

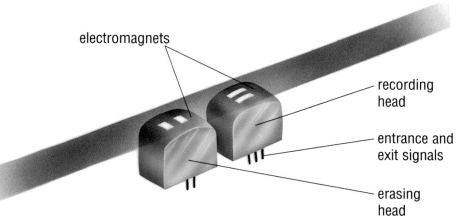

electromagnets

recording head

entrance and exit signals

erasing head

Color Television

Because of radio, television, the Internet, and other technologies, the entire world has access to instant information and images. The work of Guglielmo Marconi was important in the invention of radio and television. Television programs were first broadcast in black and white, but now most people watch color television. People can use television in a wide variety of ways. For example, space probes carry television cameras that capture images from deep space, cameras help control traffic in big cities, and cameras provide security for buildings. Television cameras record sound and light and change them into a type of invisible energy called electromagnetic waves. These waves are sent to a transmission antenna or satellite. From there, the waves are sent to homes throughout the world.

Some of the first television stars were characters from black-and-white cartoons, such as "Felix the Cat."

COLOR TELEVISION

Color television uses three beams of electrons; black-and-white television uses just one. For color broadcasts, the camera breaks down an image into three basic colors and then collects the color signals in tubes.

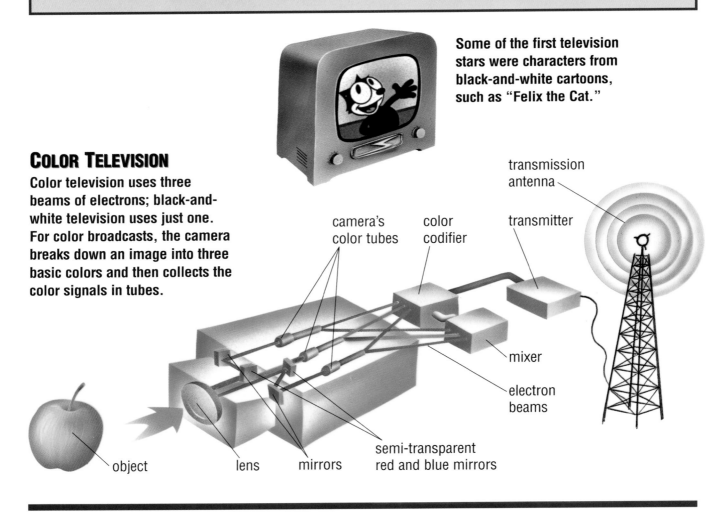

camera's color tubes

color codifier

transmission antenna

transmitter

mixer

electron beams

object

lens

mirrors

semi-transparent red and blue mirrors

EARLY TELEVISION

The first television transmissions were made through what is known as a Nipkow disk. This was a mechanical way to make the camera scan and transmit an image one line at a time to create an entire picture.

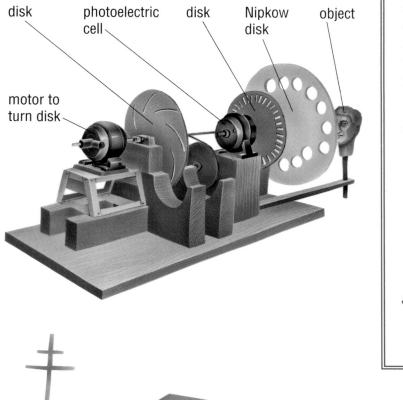

disk   photoelectric   disk   Nipkow   object
cell   disk

motor to
turn disk

antenna   receiver   color electron   deflection   shadow   screen
receiver   box/tuner   tubes   coils/baffles   mask

HOW DOES TELEVISION WORK?

Television sets receive waves sent by large transmission antennas. The waves are converted into electrical signals that change the intensity of an electron beam moving across the screen inside the television. The screen is fluorescent and has various points that are lit up by the electron beam passing across it.

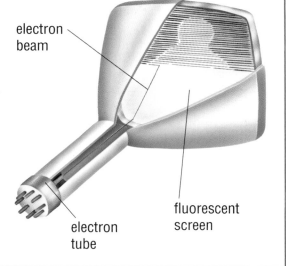

electron
beam

electron
tube

fluorescent
screen

Motion Pictures

Motion pictures, or movies, play an important role in our lives today. When we watch a movie, imaginary worlds seem almost real. In the last few years, movies have added some amazing special effects and 3-D images. The effects are often created on a computer or with the use of advanced forms of make-up. Another fascinating feature of movie-watching is semi-spherical cinema, where the spectator is in a seat reclined nearly horizontally. The screen in this type of theater measures more than 10,765 square feet (1,000 square meters)!

The pictures in semi-spherical theaters are ten times bigger than in a normal film. These theaters make the images on the screen seem completely real!

MAKING PICTURES MOVE

French brothers Louis and Auguste Lumière share credit with Thomas Edison for the invention of motion pictures in the late 1800s. Images were projected onto a screen similar to the screens used today.

IMAGES WITH DEPTH

In the first screenings of 3-D (three-dimensional) films, the audience wore special glasses. One lens was red, and the other was blue. Today, audiences use special liquid crystal glasses.

HOW DOES A MOVIE CAMERA WORK?

Movie cameras and projectors capture and project images. A movie is a swift projection of still images. Inside the camera, film is wound around a reel. When the camera is running, the film passes through a gate in the camera, where a still image is exposed. The film is then wound around an exit reel.

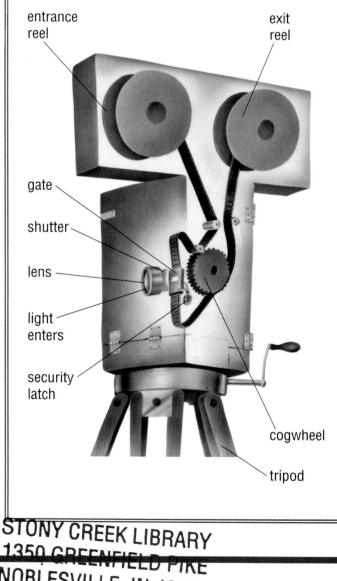

entrance reel

exit reel

gate

shutter

lens

light enters

security latch

cogwheel

tripod

The Computer

In early times, books had to be copied by hand, one by one. They were copied onto parchment by monks in monasteries. In the fifteenth century, Johannes Gutenberg invented movable type. This meant that many copies of the same book could be printed at once. The printing press was revolutionary because it brought books and knowledge to the minds of everyday people. Today, the invention of the personal computer and the technology of the Internet have allowed information to be even more available to people all around the world. Working with information containing a massive number of words has been simplified, too. For example, within a piece of writing, parts of the text can easily be moved from one place to another. The text can be corrected with the touch of a few computer keys. The personal computer also has a memory that allows it to store a very large quantity of information.

PERSONAL COMPUTER

Personal computers are becoming more and more common every day. Besides word processing, computers are helpful for using the Internet, banking, shopping, investing, doing artistic projects, e-mailing, and more.

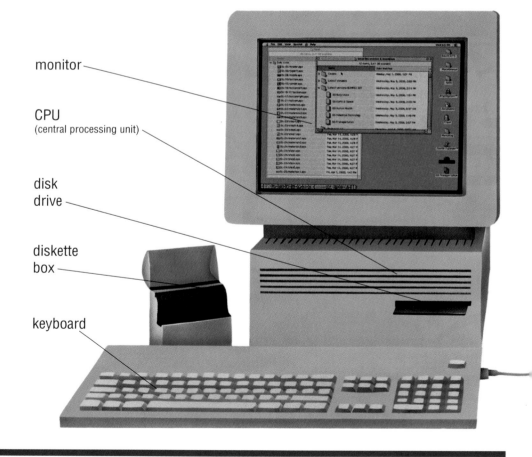

monitor

CPU
(central processing unit)

disk
drive

diskette
box

keyboard

How did the Gutenberg press work?

The Gutenberg press was very similar to the early machine that squeezed grapes to make wine. Movable metal type was set in a form for each page of a book. One page form at a time was positioned in the press. Ink was applied to the type by hand with a leather pad. A sheet of paper was laid over the inked type. Pressure printed the inked letters onto the paper. Books were printed page by page, with as many copies of each page printed as needed. The first book printed was the Bible, in Latin, in about 1456 in Mainz, Germany. Only 47 copies of this Bible exist today. Of these, three are perfect copies.

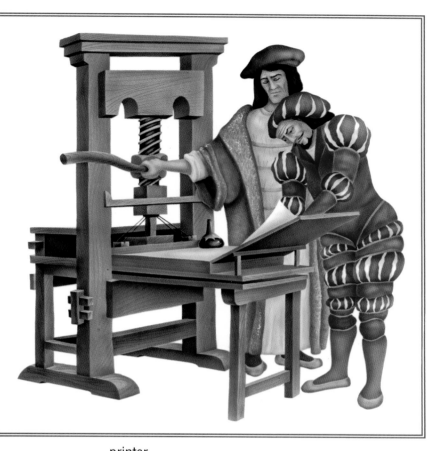

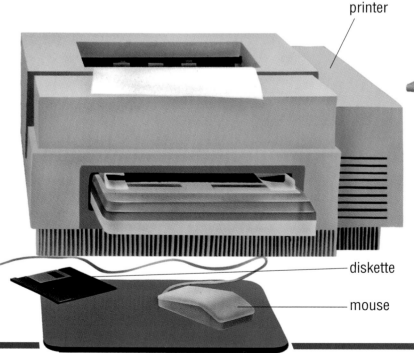

printer

diskette

mouse

The Typewriter

The first successful typewriter was invented in the nineteenth century in Milwaukee, Wisconsin. The manual machine gradually developed into the twentieth-century electric version. Some modern computerized typewriters even have memory for information storage.

Batteries

After the discovery of electricity, scientists like Michael Faraday and Alessandro Volta discovered a way to create and store electricity — the battery. In a battery, the energy of a chemical reaction is converted into electricity. Today's batteries are "dry," because they use a solid electrolyte instead of liquid. When the battery poles are connected, a chemical reaction occurs, causing the zinc to lose electrons. The electrons flow toward the manganese oxide/carbon, causing an electrical current. The dry cell came about because of the work of French chemist George Leclanché in the 1860s. Today, large wet batteries are used in automobiles.

DRY CELL BATTERY

Battery casings are made of steel. A battery like the one pictured can produce an electrical current of 1.5 volts.

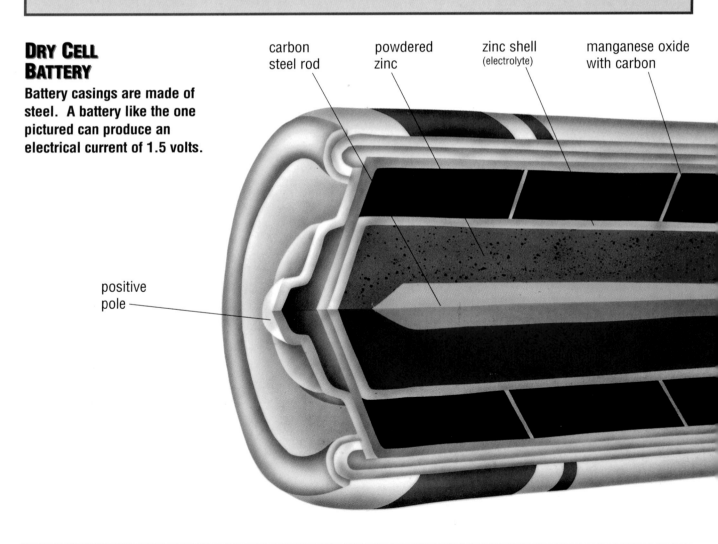

carbon steel rod

powdered zinc

zinc shell (electrolyte)

manganese oxide with carbon

positive pole

"ANIMAL ELECTRICITY"

Italian physician Luigi Galvani discovered that the legs of a frog contracted when the muscles and nerves were touched with two different metals. Alessandro Volta showed that electricity was produced by the metals and moisture, not the frog. This led to Volta's invention of the first battery.

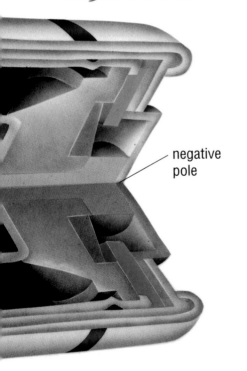

negative pole

HOW DID THE FIRST BATTERIES WORK?

The first batteries were very similar to today's batteries. Italian scientist Alessandro Volta discovered that, by putting two different metals together, electricity could be generated. The first battery was produced using this theory, alternating copper and zinc disks. Porous cardboard dipped in a saline solution was placed in between each pair of disks. The zinc and copper disks were joined by a conductor cable, and electricity was generated.

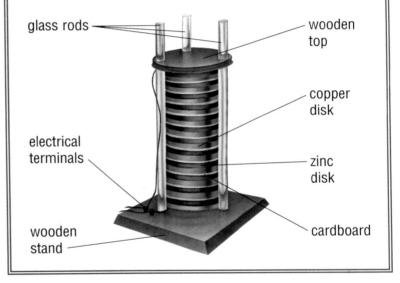

glass rods — wooden top — copper disk — electrical terminals — zinc disk — wooden stand — cardboard

WATCH BATTERY

In watch batteries *(right)*, the current is produced by powdered zinc and mercury oxide.

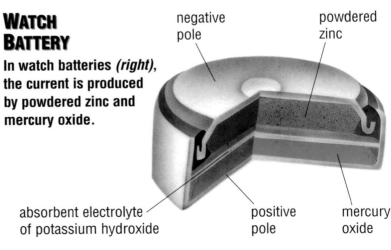

negative pole — powdered zinc — absorbent electrolyte of potassium hydroxide — positive pole — mercury oxide

The Water Meter

A water meter measures the water consumed by a household. Every time someone turns on the tap, the flowing water turns a wheel, and a gear meshes with another gear. These gear wheels mesh with others, the last of which is called the meter wheel. In this way, the water meter measures the number of gallons (liters) of water consumed. Gas pump meters use the same system as water meters. Both of these meters are descendants of the ancient water clocks that indicated the time through the movement of water.

HOW DID THE CLEPSYDRA WORK?

Ancient water clocks, or clepsydras, are the ancestors of modern water meters. A clepsydra consisted of a figurine standing on top of a rod connected to a float. As the float rose in a container of water, the figure also rose and indicated the time on a cylinder. Each hour, water entered the container from a reservoir. Because of the siphon effect, the water flowed from the container and emptied into a drum compartment. The weight of the water turned the drum. Through the gear mechanism, the turning drum also turned the hour cylinder. Greeks in ancient Athens timed speeches with clepsydras.

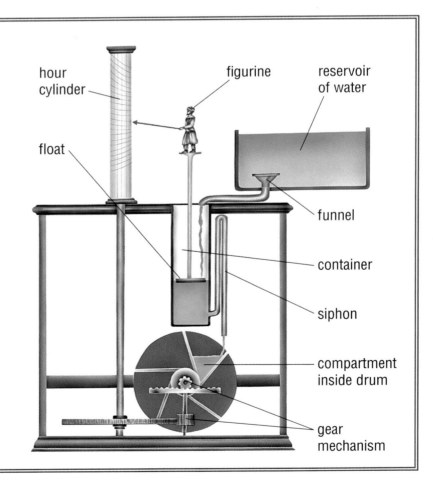

hour cylinder

figurine

reservoir of water

float

funnel

container

siphon

compartment inside drum

gear mechanism

GAS PUMP

In gas pumps, liquid turns gears similar to those in water meters. This mechanism descended from the ancient clepsydras.

CHINESE WATER CLOCK

In a Chinese water clock, water dripped slowly from a hole. The water level dropped to various marks inside the container, indicating the time.

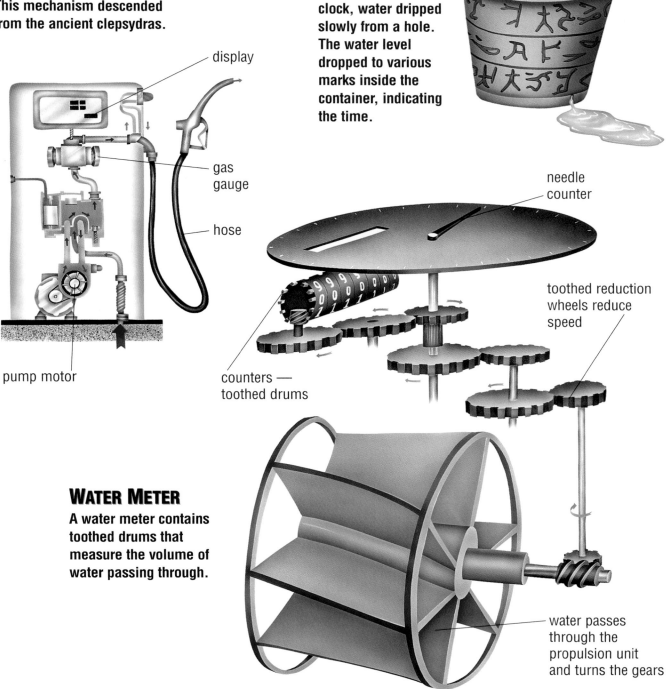

display

gas gauge

hose

pump motor

needle counter

toothed reduction wheels reduce speed

counters — toothed drums

WATER METER

A water meter contains toothed drums that measure the volume of water passing through.

water passes through the propulsion unit and turns the gears

Making a Candle Clock

YOU WILL NEED:

modeling clay

thread

weight

metal tray and a plate

candle

watch

pins

ruler

In earlier times, some people told the time by burning candles. The passage of time was marked by how long it took a candle to burn down. To determine a lengthy period of time, they arranged several candles in a line. The principle is illustrated in this project. Be very careful when working with candles because of the fire hazard.
DO THIS PROJECT ONLY WITH AN ADULT PRESENT.

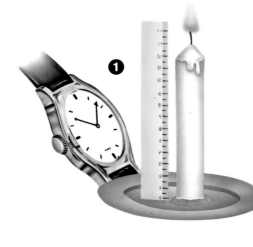

1. Attach the candle to a plate with modeling clay. Light the candle and calculate, with a ruler, how much of the candle burns away in fifteen minutes.

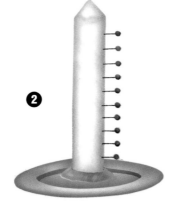

2. Stick some pins into the candle *(as shown)*. The distance between pins should be equal to the distance calculated in Step 1.

3. With identical distances between each pin, one pin should fall for every fifteen minutes of burning.

4. To make a candle alarm clock, tie a thread around the pin in the candle where you want to remember that it's dinner time.

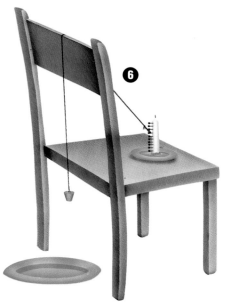

5. Put the plate on a chair and the thread over the back of the chair. Tie a weight to the end of the thread.

❺

6. Place a metal tray on the floor, just below the weight.

❻

7. When the flame reaches the thread, the pin will pull out, taking the thread with it. The weight will then fall onto the metal tray. The sound of the weight hitting the tray acts as an alarm to get your attention.

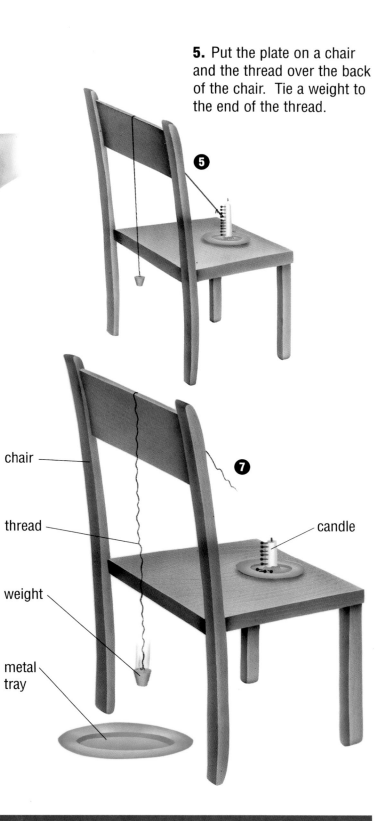

chair

thread

❼

candle

weight

metal tray

Creating a Magnetic Field

YOU WILL NEED:

insulated wire

compass

two screws

battery

flat piece of wood

One day when Hans Christian Oersted was teaching a class, he saw that electricity moved a compass needle. A compass needle's magnetized red end will naturally be attracted to the north pole of Earth. Electricity sets up a different magnetic field from Earth's. Do the project below to see for yourself that electricity produces a magnetic field.

1. Secure two wood screws into a board, about 4 inches (10 centimeters) apart. Ask an adult to help.

2. Tie the wire tightly between the two screws. Tie two knots at the top of each screw. Leave a length of wire dangling at both ends.

3. Place a compass underneath the wire. Position the wood so that the needle of the compass is parallel to the wire *(as shown)*.

4. Connect one end of the wire to the positive terminal of the battery. Connect the other end to the negative terminal.

5. Watch how the needle of the compass moves.

Pendulums

YOU WILL NEED:

plastic ruler

thread

glass rod

wool and silk cloth

two corks or cork balls

stick

Electricity is produced because electrons move from one body to another when they are rubbed together. In this experiment, the ruler becomes negatively charged and the glass rod becomes positively charged. That is the reason why the cork balls with the opposite charge attract each other, and the cork balls with the same charge repel each other.

1. Tie a piece of thread to each ball of cork. Hang the balls on a stick just a few inches (cm) apart from each other.

2. Rub the ruler with the wool cloth, and the glass rod with the silk cloth to create static electricity.

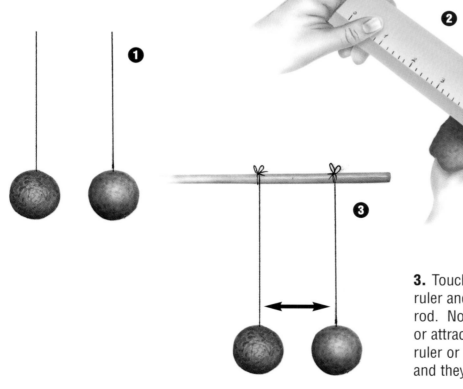

3. Touch one of the cork balls with the ruler and the other ball with the glass rod. Notice how the balls move together, or attract. Touch both balls with the ruler or both balls with the glass rod, and they move away, or repel.

Working with Sound Waves

YOU WILL NEED:

wind-up clock

porcelain plate

newspaper

When an object vibrates, it makes a sound. The vibrations produce waves that travel through air. The waves are reflected or absorbed, depending on what kind of surface they hit. Do the project below to see for yourself how the exact same sound can either be reflected or absorbed. You'll see why echoes happen in rocky canyons.

1. Roll up two pieces of newspaper to make tubes 1 inch (2.5 cm) in diameter. Tape them securely. Put the tubes on top of a table in a V shape, but not touching each other. The tubes should overhang the table at the point where they are closest.

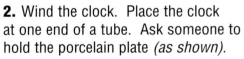

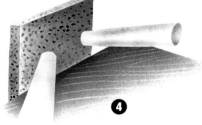

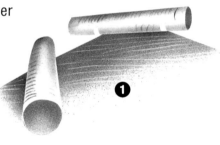

2. Wind the clock. Place the clock at one end of a tube. Ask someone to hold the porcelain plate *(as shown)*.

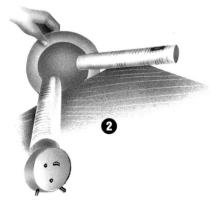

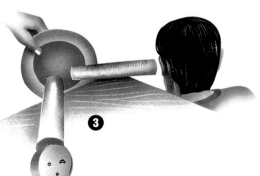

4. Replace the plate with an object that will absorb the sound waves, such as a piece of cork, a sponge, or a folded towel. When you again put your ear next to the tube, you will not hear the clock as clearly.

3. Put your ear next to the end of the tube that does not lead to the clock. You will hear the clock ticking.

YOU WILL NEED:

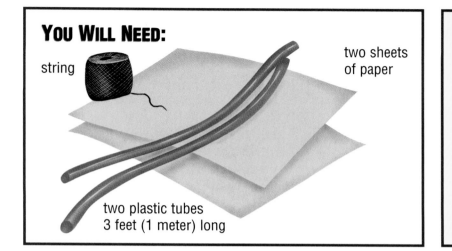

string

two sheets of paper

two plastic tubes
3 feet (1 meter) long

When we hear a sound, we can usually tell where the sound waves are coming from. There is a small time difference between when the sound is made and when it reaches our ears, and the brain can compare signals from our two ears to determine the origin of the sound. Do the project below to see for yourself how the brain can sometimes be tricked.

1. Tie the two tubes together, *(as shown).*

❷

❶

2. Make two funnels with the sheets of paper. Tape them securely to the bottom ends of the tubes.

❸

3. Place the other two ends of the tubes in your ears. Ask a friend to stand to one side and make a noise. With this device, the sound will seem to be coming from the opposite side.

Making a Camera

YOU WILL NEED:

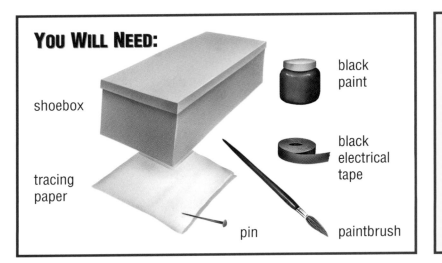

shoebox

tracing paper

pin

black paint

black electrical tape

paintbrush

A movie camera is basically the same as a still photographic camera. The main difference is that the movie camera produces ten or more photographs a second to the still camera's one. To make a movie, you must print each one of the stills. Do the project below to make your own pin-hole still camera. Then search the Internet for pin-hole photos.

1. Paint the inside of the shoebox and lid with black paint.

❶

2. Poke a small hole in one of the ends of the shoebox with a pin *(as shown)*.

❷

❸

3. At the opposite end of the shoebox from the hole, cut out a square with scissors *(as shown)*.

4. Cut a piece of tracing paper that is larger than the square. Place the paper over the square in the shoebox, and tape it in place with black electrical tape.

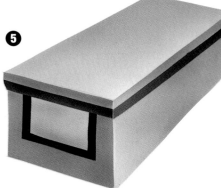

5. Put the lid back on the box. Tape the lid securely in place with black electrical tape so light cannot enter.

6. Point the small hole in the box at any object. Look through the paper, and you will see the object reflected, upside down!

Glossary

amplitude: the height of a wave, such as a radio carrier wave.

antenna: a wire or rod used to send or receive radio waves.

atom: the smallest particle of an element that has the same chemical properties as that element.

capacitor: a device that stores electrical current generated elsewhere.

circuit: the complete, continuous path of an electrical current.

cogwheel: a toothed wheel, or gear.

compass: a device that contains a freely turning needle that always points to magnetic north.

digital: of or relating to information shown in numerical characters.

electrolyte: a substance that, when dissolved in a suitable solvent or when fused, becomes a conductor of ions and is able to conduct electricity.

electromagnet: magnetic material surrounded by a coil of wire through which an electrical current can pass to magnetize the core.

electrons: negatively charged electric particles. Electrons orbit an atom's nucleus.

gear mechanism: a device that transmits movement through the use of cogwheels that interlock and turn.

generator: a machine that changes mechanical energy into electrical energy.

laser: a device that makes light waves stronger and then concentrates them into an intense beam.

Leyden jar: an early device that stored static electricity. It consisted of a glass jar partly filled with water and then corked. The cork was pierced with a nail that dipped into the water. Through the nail, static electricity was transmitted into the jar and stored. Modern versions of the Leyden jar are coated with metal foil.

nucleus: an atom's center, made up of positive protons and uncharged neutrons.

oscillator: a device for producing alternating current; a radio-frequency or audio-frequency generator.

pendulum: an object that swings freely on a vertical plane. It is influenced by gravity.

quartz: an extremely hard mineral that is transparent and of many different colors. It can be found in rock or on its own.

semiconductor: any of a group of solids, such as germanium and silicon, whose ability to conduct electricity lies between that of a conductor and that of an insulator. A semiconductor can carry electricity at high temperatures, but at low temperatures it does not.

siphon effect: the use of air pressure and suction to create a continuous flow and exchange of a liquid.

static electricity: stationary charges of electricity; electricity at rest, as opposed to an electric current.

torsion: the degree, or amount, of twisting or wrenching of an object around its own axis, usually with one end fastened tightly.

transistor: an electrical device made of a small block of a semiconductor. It amplifies an electrical current.

zinc: a white-blue metal used in industry. It protects objects from rusting. In dry batteries, zinc is the negative electrode; a mixture of zinc chloride with ammonium chloride forms the electrolyte, which is the source of electrons that produce electricity.

More Books to Read

Computer Dictionary for Beginners. Anna Claybourne (EDC)

Electricity. Simon De Pinna (Raintree/Steck Vaughn)

Keeping Time: From the Beginning and into the 21st Century. Franklyn M. Branley (Houghton Mifflin)

Machines and Inventions. Record Breakers (series). Peter Lafferty (Gareth Stevens)

Measure up with Science (series). Brenda Walpole (Gareth Stevens)

Movies. Chris Oxlade and Julian Rowe (Heineman Library)

Science Works! (series). Steve Parker (Gareth Stevens)

The Story of Writing and Printing. Anita Ganeri (Evans Brothers, Ltd.)

Television: What's Behind What You See. W. Carter Merbreier and Linda Riley (Farrar, Straus & Giroux)

Young Scientist Concepts & Projects (series). (Gareth Stevens)

Videos to Watch

The Amazing Internet. (Library Video)

The Computer. (Hawkhill)

Dry Batteries and Light Bulbs. (Films for the Humanities and Sciences)

Electric Currents and Circuits. (MTI Films)

Magnetism. (United Learning)

Marconi: Whisper in the Air. (Moonbeam)

Radio Studio. (First Light Video)

The Transistor. (Films for the Humanities and Sciences)

Video Biographies: Scientists and Inventors. (AIMS Multimedia)

Web Sites to Visit

web.mit.edu/invent/

mustang.coled.umn.edu/inventing/
  inventing.html

www.yahooligans.com/Science_and_Nature/
  Computer_Science/

www.invent.org/book/index.html

Some web sites stay current longer than others. For further web sites, use your search engines to locate the following topics: *batteries, clepsydras, clocks, computers, Thomas Edison, electricity, electromagnets, inventions, inventors, magnetic fields, radio, television,* and *transistors.*

Index